MULTNOMAH

This planner belongs to:

_____

_____

_____

_____

THE LION CHASER'S MANIFESTO

Quit living as if the purpose of life
is to arrive safely at death.
Run to the roar.
Set God-sized goals. Pursue God-given passions.
Go after a dream that is destined to fail
without divine intervention.
Stop pointing out problems. Become part of the solution.
Stop repeating the past. Start creating the future.
Face your fears. Fight for your dreams.
Grab opportunity by the mane and don't let go!
Live like today is the first day and last day of your life.
Burn sinful bridges. Blaze new trails.
Live for the applause of nail-scarred hands.
Don't let what's wrong with you
keep you from worshiping what's right with God.
Dare to fail. Dare to be different.
Quit holding out. Quit holding back. Quit running away.

CHASE THE LION.

Dear Lion Chaser,

In 2017, I accomplished one of my life goals by finishing the Chicago marathon. When I set that goal, it seemed impossible. I could barely run 3 miles, and I'm using the word "run" loosely! So, what did I do? I just went out and tried running 26.2 miles one day. No, no, I didn't. I would not have made it very far! What I actually did was download a training plan that broke that life goal into smaller steps. Over eighteen weeks, I did 72 training runs totaling nearly 500 miles.

I want you to think of this weekly planner as your training plan. I don't know what lion you're chasing, what goal you're going after. But I do know that goals are dreams with deadlines. You have to break your goal into manageable and measurable steps. Then you put one foot in front of the other, one day at a time. A weekly planner not only helps you chart a course and track your progress, but it also leaves a trail for others to follow.

At the end of this planner, you'll have the opportunity to write your very own lion chaser's manifesto. Then I outline the seven steps to setting life goals, and I also share my own life goal list. Why? Because I want to give you an example to follow. When I created my first life goal list almost twenty years ago, I studied other people's lists. Yes, I stole a few ideas. But I also found a way to put my own unique twist on them. For example, lots of people want to visit the Eiffel Tower in Paris, France. My goal? To kiss my wife, Lora, on top of it.

I hope my list inspires some ideas of your own. Feel free to beg, borrow, and steal. But your life goal list—and your manifesto—should be as unique as you are. You will chart a unique course, and God will order your footsteps along the way!

Please don't underestimate the significance of what you're about to do. Goal setting is good stewardship! Hebrews 11:1 says, "Faith is the assurance of things hoped for." Isn't that precisely what a goal is?

As the lion chaser's manifesto says, "Set God-sized goals. Pursue God-given passions. Go after a dream that is destined to fail without divine intervention."

Run to the roar!

HOW TO USE
THIS PLANNER

If you've read my book *Chase the Lion* (or even if you haven't!), you know how hard it can be to pursue your goals and dreams relentlessly. If you're like me, you've been inspired to believe that "the only way to tap your God-given potential, to fulfill your God-ordained destiny, is to chase five-hundred-pound lions." Yet, you may be wondering how to begin. That's why the *Chase the Lion Weekly Planner* was created. This tool will equip you to establish priorities and put timelines to your God-sized dreams so that you have a strategic plan for your life and can track your progress. With twelve undated monthly calendars and five weekly pages in between, the *Chase the Lion Weekly Planner* will help you thrive while keeping you organized. You'll also have the opportunity to identify the lions you intend to chase, record your goals, and write your very own lion chaser's manifesto. Remember: "Destiny is not a mystery, destiny is a decision."

MONTHLY CALENDAR PAGES

Each month begins with a customizable month-at-a-glance planning page. You'll be able to plan your month and note important dates and deadlines. In addition, we have provided monthly prompts that will equip you to write your very own lion chaser's manifesto at the end of a year. Taking the time to answer and reflect on these questions each month can help you pay attention to what God has planned for you, now and in the future. How can you pursue your dreams this month to walk the path of God's purpose for you?

WEEKLY PLANNING PAGES

Each customizable weekly spread features an inspiring quote from *Chase the Lion* and space to record your to-do lists for the week, inspiring prayers or Scripture, small and large goals, and God-sized dreams.

- **LIONS TO CHASE THIS WEEK** Make to-do lists so you can check items off as you accomplish them and record your small-scale goals

- **WEEKLY INSPIRATION** Write down Scripture verses or prayers that will motivate you to chase your lion!

- **GOD-SIZED DREAMS** Keep track of your large-scale dreams, monthly or yearly ongoing goals, or the big dreams God has inspired you to achieve

- **LIONS CHASED THIS WEEK** Don't forget to highlight the items you accomplished this week and any progress you made toward your goals

- **SCRATCH PAD** Each weekly spread includes plenty of blank spaces for recording your appointments, shopping lists, prayers, books to read, or any other information you want to remember

· · ·

In addition to the weekly and monthly planning pages, the *Chase the Lion Weekly Planner* walks you through the process of writing your own lion chaser's manifesto and your top 100 life goals. Additional features include blank bullet journal pages and year-at-a-glance calendars for multiple years.

I pray this planner helps unleash your faith and courage so that you can identify, chase, and catch the five-hundred-pound dreams in your life. Quit playing it safe and start running toward the roar!

2019

JANUARY
S	M	T	W	T	F	S
		1	2	3	4	5
6	7	8	9	10	11	12
13	14	15	16	17	18	19
20	21	22	23	24	25	26
27	28	29	30	31		

FEBRUARY
S	M	T	W	T	F	S
					1	2
3	4	5	6	7	8	9
10	11	12	13	14	15	16
17	18	19	20	21	22	23
24	25	26	27	28		

MARCH
S	M	T	W	T	F	S
					1	2
3	4	5	6	7	8	9
10	11	12	13	14	15	16
17	18	19	20	21	22	23
24	25	26	27	28	29	30
31						

APRIL
S	M	T	W	T	F	S
	1	2	3	4	5	6
7	8	9	10	11	12	13
14	15	16	17	18	19	20
21	22	23	24	25	26	27
28	29	30				

MAY
S	M	T	W	T	F	S
			1	2	3	4
5	6	7	8	9	10	11
12	13	14	15	16	17	18
19	20	21	22	23	24	25
26	27	28	29	30	31	

JUNE
S	M	T	W	T	F	S
						1
2	3	4	5	6	7	8
9	10	11	12	13	14	15
16	17	18	19	20	21	22
23	24	25	26	27	28	29
30						

JULY
S	M	T	W	T	F	S
	1	2	3	4	5	6
7	8	9	10	11	12	13
14	15	16	17	18	19	20
21	22	23	24	25	26	27
28	29	30	31			

AUGUST
S	M	T	W	T	F	S
				1	2	3
4	5	6	7	8	9	10
11	12	13	14	15	16	17
18	19	20	21	22	23	24
25	26	27	28	29	30	31

SEPTEMBER
S	M	T	W	T	F	S
1	2	3	4	5	6	7
8	9	10	11	12	13	14
15	16	17	18	19	20	21
22	23	24	25	26	27	28
29	30					

OCTOBER
S	M	T	W	T	F	S
		1	2	3	4	5
6	7	8	9	10	11	12
13	14	15	16	17	18	19
20	21	22	23	24	25	26
27	28	29	30	31		

NOVEMBER
S	M	T	W	T	F	S
					1	2
3	4	5	6	7	8	9
10	11	12	13	14	15	16
17	18	19	20	21	22	23
24	25	26	27	28	29	30

DECEMBER
S	M	T	W	T	F	S
1	2	3	4	5	6	7
8	9	10	11	12	13	14
15	16	17	18	19	20	21
22	23	24	25	26	27	28
29	30	31				

2020

JANUARY
S	M	T	W	T	F	S
			1	2	3	4
5	6	7	8	9	10	11
12	13	14	15	16	17	18
19	20	21	22	23	24	25
26	27	28	29	30	31	

FEBRUARY
S	M	T	W	T	F	S
						1
2	3	4	5	6	7	8
9	10	11	12	13	14	15
16	17	18	19	20	21	22
23	24	25	26	27	28	29

MARCH
S	M	T	W	T	F	S
1	2	3	4	5	6	7
8	9	10	11	12	13	14
15	16	17	18	19	20	21
22	23	24	25	26	27	28
29	30	31				

APRIL
S	M	T	W	T	F	S
			1	2	3	4
5	6	7	8	9	10	11
12	13	14	15	16	17	18
19	20	21	22	23	24	25
26	27	28	29	30		

MAY
S	M	T	W	T	F	S
					1	2
3	4	5	6	7	8	9
10	11	12	13	14	15	16
17	18	19	20	21	22	23
24	25	26	27	28	29	30
31						

JUNE
S	M	T	W	T	F	S
	1	2	3	4	5	6
7	8	9	10	11	12	13
14	15	16	17	18	19	20
21	22	23	24	25	26	27
28	29	30				

JULY
S	M	T	W	T	F	S
			1	2	3	4
5	6	7	8	9	10	11
12	13	14	15	16	17	18
19	20	21	22	23	24	25
26	27	28	29	30	31	

AUGUST
S	M	T	W	T	F	S
						1
2	3	4	5	6	7	8
9	10	11	12	13	14	15
16	17	18	19	20	21	22
23	24	25	26	27	28	29
30	31					

SEPTEMBER
S	M	T	W	T	F	S
		1	2	3	4	5
6	7	8	9	10	11	12
13	14	15	16	17	18	19
20	21	22	23	24	25	26
27	28	29	30			

OCTOBER
S	M	T	W	T	F	S
				1	2	3
4	5	6	7	8	9	10
11	12	13	14	15	16	17
18	19	20	21	22	23	24
25	26	27	28	29	30	31

NOVEMBER
S	M	T	W	T	F	S
1	2	3	4	5	6	7
8	9	10	11	12	13	14
15	16	17	18	19	20	21
22	23	24	25	26	27	28
29	30					

DECEMBER
S	M	T	W	T	F	S
		1	2	3	4	5
6	7	8	9	10	11	12
13	14	15	16	17	18	19
20	21	22	23	24	25	26
27	28	29	30	31		

2021

JANUARY
S	M	T	W	T	F	S
					1	2
3	4	5	6	7	8	9
10	11	12	13	14	15	16
17	18	19	20	21	22	23
24	25	26	27	28	29	30
31						

FEBRUARY
S	M	T	W	T	F	S
	1	2	3	4	5	6
7	8	9	10	11	12	13
14	15	16	17	18	19	20
21	22	23	24	25	26	27
28						

MARCH
S	M	T	W	T	F	S
	1	2	3	4	5	6
7	8	9	10	11	12	13
14	15	16	17	18	19	20
21	22	23	24	25	26	27
28	29	30	31			

APRIL
S	M	T	W	T	F	S
				1	2	3
4	5	6	7	8	9	10
11	12	13	14	15	16	17
18	19	20	21	22	23	24
25	26	27	28	29	30	

MAY
S	M	T	W	T	F	S
						1
2	3	4	5	6	7	8
9	10	11	12	13	14	15
16	17	18	19	20	21	22
23	24	25	26	27	28	29
30	31					

JUNE
S	M	T	W	T	F	S
		1	2	3	4	5
6	7	8	9	10	11	12
13	14	15	16	17	18	19
20	21	22	23	24	25	26
27	28	29	30			

JULY
S	M	T	W	T	F	S
				1	2	3
4	5	6	7	8	9	10
11	12	13	14	15	16	17
18	19	20	21	22	23	24
25	26	27	28	29	30	31

AUGUST
S	M	T	W	T	F	S
1	2	3	4	5	6	7
8	9	10	11	12	13	14
15	16	17	18	19	20	21
22	23	24	25	26	27	28
29	30	31				

SEPTEMBER
S	M	T	W	T	F	S
			1	2	3	4
5	6	7	8	9	10	11
12	13	14	15	16	17	18
19	20	21	22	23	24	25
26	27	28	29	30		

OCTOBER
S	M	T	W	T	F	S
					1	2
3	4	5	6	7	8	9
10	11	12	13	14	15	16
17	18	19	20	21	22	23
24	25	26	27	28	29	30
31						

NOVEMBER
S	M	T	W	T	F	S
	1	2	3	4	5	6
7	8	9	10	11	12	13
14	15	16	17	18	19	20
21	22	23	24	25	26	27
28	29	30				

DECEMBER
S	M	T	W	T	F	S
			1	2	3	4
5	6	7	8	9	10	11
12	13	14	15	16	17	18
19	20	21	22	23	24	25
26	27	28	29	30	31	

2022

JANUARY
S	M	T	W	T	F	S
						1
2	3	4	5	6	7	8
9	10	11	12	13	14	15
16	17	18	19	20	21	22
23	24	25	26	27	28	29
30	31					

FEBRUARY
S	M	T	W	T	F	S
		1	2	3	4	5
6	7	8	9	10	11	12
13	14	15	16	17	18	19
20	21	22	23	24	25	26
27	28					

MARCH
S	M	T	W	T	F	S
		1	2	3	4	5
6	7	8	9	10	11	12
13	14	15	16	17	18	19
20	21	22	23	24	25	26
27	28	29	30	31		

APRIL
S	M	T	W	T	F	S
					1	2
3	4	5	6	7	8	9
10	11	12	13	14	15	16
17	18	19	20	21	22	23
24	25	26	27	28	29	30

MAY
S	M	T	W	T	F	S
1	2	3	4	5	6	7
8	9	10	11	12	13	14
15	16	17	18	19	20	21
22	23	24	25	26	27	28
29	30	31				

JUNE
S	M	T	W	T	F	S
			1	2	3	4
5	6	7	8	9	10	11
12	13	14	15	16	17	18
19	20	21	22	23	24	25
26	27	28	29	30		

JULY
S	M	T	W	T	F	S
					1	2
3	4	5	6	7	8	9
10	11	12	13	14	15	16
17	18	19	20	21	22	23
24	25	26	27	28	29	30
31						

AUGUST
S	M	T	W	T	F	S
	1	2	3	4	5	6
7	8	9	10	11	12	13
14	15	16	17	18	19	20
21	22	23	24	25	26	27
28	29	30	31			

SEPTEMBER
S	M	T	W	T	F	S
				1	2	3
4	5	6	7	8	9	10
11	12	13	14	15	16	17
18	19	20	21	22	23	24
25	26	27	28	29	30	

OCTOBER
S	M	T	W	T	F	S
						1
2	3	4	5	6	7	8
9	10	11	12	13	14	15
16	17	18	19	20	21	22
23	24	25	26	27	28	29
30	31					

NOVEMBER
S	M	T	W	T	F	S
		1	2	3	4	5
6	7	8	9	10	11	12
13	14	15	16	17	18	19
20	21	22	23	24	25	26
27	28	29	30			

DECEMBER
S	M	T	W	T	F	S
				1	2	3
4	5	6	7	8	9	10
11	12	13	14	15	16	17
18	19	20	21	22	23	24
25	26	27	28	29	30	31

MONTH:

SUNDAY	MONDAY	TUESDAY	WEDNESDAY

THURSDAY	FRIDAY	SATURDAY

RUN TO THE ROAR
MANIFESTO

WHAT THREE
ADJECTIVES
DESCRIBE HOW
YOU WANT TO
LIVE YOUR LIFE
THIS YEAR?

MONTH:

LIONS TO CHASE

MONDAY _____

INSPIRATION

TUESDAY _____

GOD-SIZED DREAMS

WEDNESDAY _____

YOU ARE ONE IDEA, ONE RISK, ONE DECISION AWAY FROM A TOTALLY DIFFERENT LIFE.

HURSDAY ＿＿＿＿＿＿

LIONS CHASED

RIDAY ＿＿＿＿＿＿

SCRATCH PAD

ATURDAY ＿＿＿＿＿＿

SUNDAY ＿＿＿＿＿＿

MONTH:

LIONS TO CHASE

MONDAY _____

INSPIRATION

TUESDAY _____

GOD-SIZED DREAMS

WEDNESDAY _____

ARE YOU LIVING YOUR LIFE IN A WAY THAT IS WORTH TELLING STORIES ABOUT?

THURSDAY _____

LIONS CHASED

FRIDAY _____

SCRATCH PAD

SATURDAY _____

SUNDAY _____

LIONS TO CHASE

MONDAY _____

INSPIRATION

TUESDAY _____

GOD-SIZED DREAMS

WEDNESDAY _____

THIS COULD BE THE GREATEST YEAR OF YOUR LIFE, YOUR DREAM YEAR, BUT YOU HAVE TO <u>WIN THE DAY</u>.

THURSDAY _____

LIONS CHASED

FRIDAY _____

SCRATCH PAD

SATURDAY _____

SUNDAY _____

LIONS TO CHASE

INSPIRATION

GOD-SIZED DREAMS

MONDAY _____

TUESDAY _____

WEDNESDAY _____

THURSDAY _____

FRIDAY _____

SATURDAY _____

SUNDAY _____

LIONS CHASED

SCRATCH PAD

MONTH:

LIONS TO CHASE

MONDAY _____

INSPIRATION

TUESDAY _____

GOD-SIZED DREAMS

WEDNESDAY _____

UNTIL YOU CAN SELFLESSLY INVEST YOURSELF IN SOMEONE ELSE'S DREAM, YOU'RE NOT READY FOR YOUR OWN.

THURSDAY _____

LIONS CHASED

FRIDAY _____

SCRATCH PAD

SATURDAY _____

SUNDAY _____

MONTH:

SUNDAY	MONDAY	TUESDAY	WEDNESDAY

THURSDAY	FRIDAY	SATURDAY

RUN TO THE ROAR
MANIFESTO

WHAT TRAITS
DO YOU NEED
TO CULTIVATE TO
PURSUE YOUR
GOD-SIZED
DREAMS?

LIONS TO CHASE

MONDAY _____

INSPIRATION

TUESDAY _____

GOD-SIZED DREAMS

WEDNESDAY _____

A GOD-SIZED DREAM WILL BE BEYOND YOUR ABILITY, BEYOND YOUR
RESOURCES. UNLESS GOD DOES IT, IT CAN'T BE DONE!

THURSDAY _____

LIONS CHASED

FRIDAY _____

SCRATCH PAD

SATURDAY _____

SUNDAY _____

MONTH:

LIONS TO CHASE

MONDAY _____

INSPIRATION

TUESDAY _____

GOD-SIZED DREAMS

WEDNESDAY _____

THURSDAY _____

LIONS CHASED

FRIDAY _____

SCRATCH PAD

SATURDAY _____

SUNDAY _____

MONTH:

LIONS TO CHASE

MONDAY _____

INSPIRATION

TUESDAY _____

GOD-SIZED DREAMS

WEDNESDAY _____

THURSDAY _____

LIONS CHASED

FRIDAY _____

SCRATCH PAD

SATURDAY _____

SUNDAY _____

LIONS TO CHASE

MONDAY _____

INSPIRATION

TUESDAY _____

GOD-SIZED DREAMS

WEDNESDAY _____

IF YOU WANT GOD TO DO SOMETHING BEYOND YOUR ABILITY, TRY GIVING BEYOND YOUR MEANS.

THURSDAY _____

LIONS CHASED

FRIDAY _____

SCRATCH PAD

SATURDAY _____

SUNDAY _____

LIONS TO CHASE

MONDAY _____

INSPIRATION

TUESDAY _____

GOD-SIZED DREAMS

WEDNESDAY _____

THURSDAY _____

LIONS CHASED

FRIDAY _____

SCRATCH PAD

SATURDAY _____

SUNDAY _____

MONTH:

SUNDAY	MONDAY	TUESDAY	WEDNESDAY

NAME A FEAR
THAT YOU NO
LONGER WANT
TO HOLD YOU
BACK. WHAT
STEPS CAN YOU
TAKE TO FACE
YOUR FEAR AND
BEGIN MOVING
FORWARD?

MONTH:

LIONS TO CHASE

MONDAY _____

INSPIRATION

TUESDAY _____

GOD-SIZED DREAMS

WEDNESDAY _____

THURSDAY _____

LIONS CHASED

FRIDAY _____

SCRATCH PAD

SATURDAY _____

SUNDAY _____

LIONS TO CHASE

MONDAY _____

INSPIRATION

TUESDAY _____

GOD-SIZED DREAMS

WEDNESDAY _____

MOST OF US SPEND OUR LIVES RUNNING AWAY FROM THE THINGS WE'RE AFRAID OF.

THURSDAY _____

LIONS CHASED

FRIDAY _____

SCRATCH PAD

SATURDAY _____

SUNDAY _____

LIONS TO CHASE

MONDAY _____

INSPIRATION

TUESDAY _____

GOD-SIZED DREAMS

WEDNESDAY _____

YOU CAN'T STEAL SECOND BASE IF YOU KEEP YOUR FOOT ON FIRST.

THURSDAY _____

LIONS CHASED

FRIDAY _____

SCRATCH PAD

SATURDAY _____

SUNDAY _____

MONTH:

LIONS TO CHASE

MONDAY _____

INSPIRATION

TUESDAY _____

GOD-SIZED DREAMS

WEDNESDAY _____

WHEN WE FAIL TO TAKE ACTION, WE FORFEIT THE FUTURE. AND JUST AS INACTION IS AN ACTION, INDECISION IS A DECISION.

THURSDAY _____

LIONS CHASED

FRIDAY _____

SCRATCH PAD

SATURDAY _____

SUNDAY _____

LIONS TO CHASE

MONDAY _____

INSPIRATION

TUESDAY _____

GOD-SIZED DREAMS

WEDNESDAY _____

EVEN WHEN YOU HAVE A SETBACK, GOD HAS ALREADY PREPARED
YOUR COMEBACK.

THURSDAY _____

LIONS CHASED

FRIDAY _____

SCRATCH PAD

SATURDAY _____

SUNDAY _____

MONTH:

SUNDAY	MONDAY	TUESDAY	WEDNESDAY

HURSDAY	FRIDAY	SATURDAY

WHAT IS YOUR
DEFINITION
OF FAITH, AND
HOW DOES IT
PLAY OUT IN
YOUR LIFE?

MONTH:

LIONS TO CHASE

MONDAY _____

INSPIRATION

TUESDAY _____

GOD-SIZED DREAMS

WEDNESDAY _____

HURSDAY _____

LIONS CHASED

RIDAY _____

SCRATCH PAD

ATURDAY _____

SUNDAY _____

LIONS TO CHASE

MONDAY _____

INSPIRATION

TUESDAY _____

GOD-SIZED DREAMS

WEDNESDAY _____

HE DOES THINGS WE CAN'T DO SO WE CAN'T TAKE CREDIT FOR THEM.
GOD HONORS BIG DREAMS BECAUSE BIG DREAMS HONOR GOD.

THURSDAY _____

LIONS CHASED

FRIDAY _____

SCRATCH PAD

SATURDAY _____

SUNDAY _____

LIONS TO CHASE

MONDAY _____

INSPIRATION

TUESDAY _____

GOD-SIZED DREAMS

WEDNESDAY _____

THE SIZE OF YOUR DREAM MAY BE THE MOST ACCURATE MEASURE OF THE SIZE OF YOUR GOD.

THURSDAY _____

LIONS CHASED

FRIDAY _____

SCRATCH PAD

SATURDAY _____

SUNDAY _____

LIONS TO CHASE

MONDAY _____

INSPIRATION

TUESDAY _____

GOD-SIZED DREAMS

WEDNESDAY _____

THURSDAY _____

LIONS CHASED

FRIDAY _____

SCRATCH PAD

SATURDAY _____

SUNDAY _____

LIONS TO CHASE

MONDAY _____

INSPIRATION

TUESDAY _____

GOD-SIZED DREAMS

WEDNESDAY _____

THURSDAY _____

LIONS CHASED

FRIDAY _____

SCRATCH PAD

SATURDAY _____

SUNDAY _____

SUNDAY	MONDAY	TUESDAY	WEDNESDAY

HURSDAY	FRIDAY	SATURDAY

WHAT WILL YOU
DO WHEN YOU
ENCOUNTER
OBSTACLES AND
CHALLENGES?

MONTH:

LIONS TO CHASE

MONDAY _____

INSPIRATION

TUESDAY _____

GOD-SIZED DREAMS

WEDNESDAY _____

THE GOD WHO IS ABLE TO DO IMMEASURABLY MORE THAN ALL YOU CAN ASK
WILL ACCOMPLISH SOMETHING WAY BEYOND WHAT YOU CAN IMAGINE.

HURSDAY _____

LIONS CHASED

RIDAY _____

SCRATCH PAD

SATURDAY _____

SUNDAY _____

MONTH:

LIONS TO CHASE

MONDAY _____

INSPIRATION

TUESDAY _____

GOD-SIZED DREAMS

WEDNESDAY _____

GREAT CONFLICTS CULTIVATE GREAT CHARACTER.

THURSDAY _____

LIONS CHASED

FRIDAY _____

SCRATCH PAD

SATURDAY _____

SUNDAY _____

LIONS TO CHASE

MONDAY _____

INSPIRATION

TUESDAY _____

GOD-SIZED DREAMS

WEDNESDAY _____

THURSDAY _____

LIONS CHASED

FRIDAY _____

SCRATCH PAD

SATURDAY _____

SUNDAY _____

LIONS TO CHASE

MONDAY _____

INSPIRATION

TUESDAY _____

GOD-SIZED DREAMS

WEDNESDAY _____

IMPOSSIBLE ODDS SET THE STAGE FOR GOD'S GREATEST MIRACLES!

THURSDAY _____

LIONS CHASED

FRIDAY _____

SCRATCH PAD

SATURDAY _____

SUNDAY _____

MONTH:

LIONS TO CHASE

MONDAY _____

INSPIRATION

TUESDAY _____

GOD-SIZED DREAMS

WEDNESDAY _____

DON'T LET WHAT YOU CANNOT DO KEEP YOU FROM DOING WHAT YOU CAN.

THURSDAY _____

LIONS CHASED

FRIDAY _____

SCRATCH PAD

SATURDAY _____

SUNDAY _____

MONTH:

SUNDAY	MONDAY	TUESDAY	WEDNESDAY

HURSDAY	FRIDAY	SATURDAY

HOW HAVE
YOU SEIZED
OPPORTUNITIES
RECENTLY?
WHAT PUSHED
YOU TO MOVE
FORWARD?

MONTH:

DESTINY IS NOT
A COUNTERINTUITIV

LIONS TO CHASE

MONDAY _____

INSPIRATION

TUESDAY _____

GOD-SIZED DREAMS

WEDNESDAY _____

THURSDAY _____

LIONS CHASED

FRIDAY _____

SCRATCH PAD

SATURDAY _____

SUNDAY _____

LIONS TO CHASE

MONDAY _____

INSPIRATION

TUESDAY _____

GOD-SIZED DREAMS

WEDNESDAY _____

IF YOU'RE LOOKING FOR AN EXCUSE, YOU'LL ALWAYS FIND ONE. IF YOU'RE LOOKING FOR AN OPPORTUNITY, YOU'LL ALWAYS FIND ONE.

THURSDAY _____

LIONS CHASED

FRIDAY _____

SCRATCH PAD

SATURDAY _____

SUNDAY _____

MONTH:

LIONS TO CHASE

MONDAY _____

INSPIRATION

TUESDAY _____

GOD-SIZED DREAMS

WEDNESDAY _____

E FOR OPPORTUNITY. THERE ARE AMAZING OPPORTUNITIES ALL AROUND
U HAVE TO SEE THEM TO SEIZE THEM.

HURSDAY _____

LIONS CHASED

RIDAY _____

SCRATCH PAD

SATURDAY _____

SUNDAY _____

LIONS TO CHASE

MONDAY _____

INSPIRATION

TUESDAY _____

GOD-SIZED DREAMS

WEDNESDAY _____

YOU ARE ONE ENCOUNTER AWAY FROM YOUR DESTINY.

THURSDAY _____

LIONS CHASED

FRIDAY _____

SCRATCH PAD

SATURDAY _____

SUNDAY _____

LIONS TO CHASE

MONDAY _____

INSPIRATION

TUESDAY _____

GOD-SIZED DREAMS

WEDNESDAY _____

THURSDAY _____

LIONS CHASED

FRIDAY _____

SCRATCH PAD

SATURDAY _____

SUNDAY _____

SUNDAY	MONDAY	TUESDAY	WEDNESDAY

THURSDAY	FRIDAY	SATURDAY

WHAT PASSIONS
HAS GOD PLACED
IN YOUR HEART?

MONTH:

LIONS TO CHASE

MONDAY _____

INSPIRATION

TUESDAY _____

GOD-SIZED DREAMS

WEDNESDAY _____

THURSDAY _____

LIONS CHASED

FRIDAY _____

SCRATCH PAD

SATURDAY _____

SUNDAY _____

LIONS TO CHASE

MONDAY _____

INSPIRATION

TUESDAY _____

GOD-SIZED DREAMS

WEDNESDAY _____

ONE OF THE BEST WAYS TO DISCOVER YOUR DESTINY IS TO STUDY YOUR HISTORY.

THURSDAY _____

LIONS CHASED

FRIDAY _____

SCRATCH PAD

SATURDAY _____

SUNDAY _____

MONTH:

LIONS TO CHASE

MONDAY _____

INSPIRATION

TUESDAY _____

GOD-SIZED DREAMS

WEDNESDAY _____

IF YOU'RE WILLING TO FIGHT FOR IT, YOU HAVE A FIGHTING CHANCE. AND GOD WILL FIGHT FOR YOU.

THURSDAY _____

LIONS CHASED

FRIDAY _____

SCRATCH PAD

SATURDAY _____

SUNDAY _____

MONTH:

LIONS TO CHASE

MONDAY _____

INSPIRATION

TUESDAY _____

GOD-SIZED DREAMS

WEDNESDAY _____

THURSDAY _____

LIONS CHASED

FRIDAY _____

SCRATCH PAD

SATURDAY _____

SUNDAY _____

LIONS TO CHASE

MONDAY _____

INSPIRATION

TUESDAY _____

GOD-SIZED DREAMS

WEDNESDAY _____

HURSDAY _____

LIONS CHASED

RIDAY _____

SCRATCH PAD

ATURDAY _____

SUNDAY _____

SUNDAY	MONDAY	TUESDAY	WEDNESDAY

HURSDAY	FRIDAY	SATURDAY

WHAT MAKES
YOU UNIQUE
AND HOW CAN
YOU USE THOSE
QUALITIES TO
ENCOURAGE AND
SERVE OTHERS?

MONTH:

LIONS TO CHASE

MONDAY _____

INSPIRATION

TUESDAY _____

GOD-SIZED DREAMS

WEDNESDAY _____

THURSDAY _____

LIONS CHASED

FRIDAY _____

SCRATCH PAD

SATURDAY _____

SUNDAY _____

MONTH:

LIONS TO CHASE

MONDAY _____

INSPIRATION

TUESDAY _____

GOD-SIZED DREAMS

WEDNESDAY _____

THURSDAY _____

LIONS CHASED

FRIDAY _____

SCRATCH PAD

SATURDAY _____

SUNDAY _____

MONTH:

LIONS TO CHASE

MONDAY _____

INSPIRATION

TUESDAY _____

GOD-SIZED DREAMS

WEDNESDAY _____

THURSDAY _____

LIONS CHASED

FRIDAY _____

SCRATCH PAD

SATURDAY _____

SUNDAY _____

MONTH:

LIONS TO CHASE

MONDAY _____

INSPIRATION

TUESDAY _____

GOD-SIZED DREAMS

WEDNESDAY _____

NEVER UNDERESTIMATE THE POWER OF ONE ACT OF KINDNESS, ONE ACT OF COURAGE, ONE ACT OF GENEROSITY.

THURSDAY _____

LIONS CHASED

FRIDAY _____

SCRATCH PAD

SATURDAY _____

SUNDAY _____

MONTH:

LIONS TO CHASE

MONDAY _____

INSPIRATION

TUESDAY _____

GOD-SIZED DREAMS

WEDNESDAY _____

BIG DREAMS OFTEN START WITH SMALL ACTS OF KINDNESS.

THURSDAY _____

LIONS CHASED

FRIDAY _____

SCRATCH PAD

SATURDAY _____

SUNDAY _____

MONTH:

SUNDAY	MONDAY	TUESDAY	WEDNESDAY

HURSDAY	FRIDAY	SATURDAY

WHAT DO YOU
NEED TO LET GO
OF IN ORDER TO
PURSUE YOUR
DREAMS?

LIONS TO CHASE

MONDAY _____

INSPIRATION

TUESDAY _____

GOD-SIZED DREAMS

WEDNESDAY _____

REPENT OF YOUR SMALL DREAMS AND YOUR SMALL GOD—DARE TO GO AFTER A DREAM THAT IS BIGGER THAN YOU ARE.

HURSDAY _____

LIONS CHASED

RIDAY _____

SCRATCH PAD

ATURDAY _____

SUNDAY _____

LIONS TO CHASE

MONDAY _____

INSPIRATION

TUESDAY _____

GOD-SIZED DREAMS

WEDNESDAY _____

EVEN IF SOMETHING IS OUT OF YOUR CONTROL, YOU STILL CONTROL YOUR REACTION.

HURSDAY _____

LIONS CHASED

RIDAY _____

SCRATCH PAD

ATURDAY _____

SUNDAY _____

LIONS TO CHASE

MONDAY _____

INSPIRATION

TUESDAY _____

GOD-SIZED DREAMS

WEDNESDAY _____

OUR GREATEST REGRET AT THE END OF OUR LIVES WILL BE THE LIONS WE DIDN'T CHASE.

THURSDAY _____

LIONS CHASED

FRIDAY _____

SCRATCH PAD

SATURDAY _____

SUNDAY _____

LIONS TO CHASE

MONDAY _____

INSPIRATION

TUESDAY _____

GOD-SIZED DREAMS

WEDNESDAY _____

NEVER UNDERESTIMATE THE POWER OF ONE WELL-TIMED, WELL-PHRASED WORD OF ENCOURAGEMENT.

THURSDAY _____

FRIDAY _____

SATURDAY _____

SUNDAY _____

LIONS CHASED

SCRATCH PAD

MONTH:

LIONS TO CHASE

MONDAY _____

INSPIRATION

TUESDAY _____

GOD-SIZED DREAMS

WEDNESDAY _____

THURSDAY _____

LIONS CHASED

FRIDAY _____

SCRATCH PAD

SATURDAY _____

SUNDAY _____

SUNDAY	MONDAY	TUESDAY	WEDNESDAY

RUN TO THE ROAR
MANIFESTO

WHERE DO
YOU NEED
TO REDIRECT
YOUR ENERGY
IN ORDER TO
FINISH THE
YEAR STRONG?

MONTH:

LIONS TO CHASE

MONDAY _____

INSPIRATION

TUESDAY _____

GOD-SIZED DREAMS

WEDNESDAY _____

HURSDAY _____

LIONS CHASED

RIDAY _____

SCRATCH PAD

SATURDAY _____

SUNDAY _____

LIONS TO CHASE

MONDAY _____

INSPIRATION

TUESDAY _____

GOD-SIZED DREAMS

WEDNESDAY _____

THURSDAY _____

FRIDAY _____

SATURDAY _____

SUNDAY _____

LIONS CHASED

SCRATCH PAD

LIONS TO CHASE

MONDAY _____

INSPIRATION

TUESDAY _____

GOD-SIZED DREAMS

WEDNESDAY _____

GOD IS IN THE BUSINESS OF STRATEGICALLY POSITIONING US IN THE RIGHT PLACE AT THE RIGHT TIME.

THURSDAY _____

LIONS CHASED

FRIDAY _____

SCRATCH PAD

SATURDAY _____

SUNDAY _____

MONTH:

LIONS TO CHASE

MONDAY _____

INSPIRATION

TUESDAY _____

GOD-SIZED DREAMS

WEDNESDAY _____

A DREAM WITHOUT A TO-DO LIST IS CALLED A WISH LIST.

THURSDAY _____

LIONS CHASED

FRIDAY _____

SCRATCH PAD

SATURDAY _____

SUNDAY _____

MONTH:

LIONS TO CHASE

MONDAY _____

INSPIRATION

TUESDAY _____

GOD-SIZED DREAMS

WEDNESDAY _____

SUCCESS: WHEN THOSE WHO KNOW YOU BEST RESPECT YOU MOST.

THURSDAY _____

LIONS CHASED

FRIDAY _____

SCRATCH PAD

SATURDAY _____

SUNDAY _____

MONTH:

SUNDAY	MONDAY	TUESDAY	WEDNESDAY

HURSDAY	FRIDAY	SATURDAY

HOW CAN
GRATITUDE
INSPIRE YOU
FOR THE
FUTURE?

MONTH:

LIONS TO CHASE

MONDAY _____

INSPIRATION

TUESDAY _____

GOD-SIZED DREAMS

WEDNESDAY _____

DON'T UNDERESTIMATE THE POWER OF ONE COMPLIMENT.

THURSDAY _____

LIONS CHASED

FRIDAY _____

SCRATCH PAD

SATURDAY _____

SUNDAY _____

LIONS TO CHASE

MONDAY _____

INSPIRATION

TUESDAY _____

GOD-SIZED DREAMS

WEDNESDAY _____

OUR GREATEST SHORTCOMING IS NOT FEELING GOOD ENOUGH ABOUT WHAT GOD HAS DONE RIGHT.

THURSDAY _____

LIONS CHASED

FRIDAY _____

SCRATCH PAD

SATURDAY _____

SUNDAY _____

MONTH:

LIONS TO CHASE

MONDAY _____

INSPIRATION

TUESDAY _____

GOD-SIZED DREAMS

WEDNESDAY _____

DON'T PUT A PERIOD WHERE GOD PUTS A COMMA.

THURSDAY _____

FRIDAY _____

SATURDAY _____

SUNDAY _____

LIONS CHASED

SCRATCH PAD

LIONS TO CHASE

MONDAY _____

INSPIRATION

TUESDAY _____

GOD-SIZED DREAMS

WEDNESDAY _____

THURSDAY _____

LIONS CHASED

FRIDAY _____

SCRATCH PAD

SATURDAY _____

SUNDAY _____

MONTH:

LIONS TO CHASE

MONDAY _____

INSPIRATION

TUESDAY _____

GOD-SIZED DREAMS

WEDNESDAY _____

THE OPPOSITE OF LOVE IS NOT HATE. THE OPPOSITE OF LOVE IS FEAR. TRUE LOVE LEADS TO FEARLESSNESS.

HURSDAY _____

LIONS CHASED

RIDAY _____

SCRATCH PAD

SATURDAY _____

SUNDAY _____

MONTH:

SUNDAY	MONDAY	TUESDAY	WEDNESDAY

THURSDAY	FRIDAY	SATURDAY

WHAT IS YOUR DRIVING MOTIVATION EACH DAY AND HOW DOES IT AFFECT YOUR LIVING LEGACY?

LIONS TO CHASE

MONDAY _____

INSPIRATION

TUESDAY _____

GOD-SIZED DREAMS

WEDNESDAY _____

WE START DYING THE DAY WE STOP DREAMING....WE START LIVING THE DAY
WE DISCOVER A DREAM WORTH DYING FOR.

THURSDAY _____

LIONS CHASED

FRIDAY _____

SCRATCH PAD

SATURDAY _____

SUNDAY _____

LIONS TO CHASE

MONDAY _____

INSPIRATION

TUESDAY _____

GOD-SIZED DREAMS

WEDNESDAY _____

FAITH IS CLIMBING OUT ON A LIMB, CUTTING IT OFF, AND WATCHING THE TREE FALL DOWN.

THURSDAY _____

LIONS CHASED

FRIDAY _____

SCRATCH PAD

SATURDAY _____

SUNDAY _____

MONTH:

LIONS TO CHASE

MONDAY _____

INSPIRATION

TUESDAY _____

GOD-SIZED DREAMS

WEDNESDAY _____

THURSDAY _____

LIONS CHASED

FRIDAY _____

SCRATCH PAD

SATURDAY _____

SUNDAY _____

LIONS TO CHASE

MONDAY _____

INSPIRATION

TUESDAY _____

GOD-SIZED DREAMS

WEDNESDAY _____

THURSDAY _____

FRIDAY _____

SATURDAY _____

SUNDAY _____

LIONS CHASED

SCRATCH PAD

LIONS TO CHASE

MONDAY _____

INSPIRATION

TUESDAY _____

GOD-SIZED DREAMS

WEDNESDAY _____

LEGACY IS THE INFLUENCE YOUR DREAM HAS ON OTHERS EVEN AFTER YOU DIE.

HURSDAY _____

LIONS CHASED

RIDAY _____

SCRATCH PAD

SATURDAY _____

SUNDAY _____

HOW TO WRITE
YOUR OWN MANIFESTO

Now is your chance to write your very own lion chaser's manifesto. A manifesto is "a written statement declaring publicly the intentions, motives, or views of its issuer." We suggest looking back at your responses to the monthly prompts for inspiration. You might also consider the goals and dreams you recorded throughout the year. This manifesto should reflect your own dreams and desires, but also the difficulties you face. What have you struggled to overcome? What holds you back from fiercely pursuing the dreams God has laid on your heart? How do you intend to transform yourself into a lion chaser? Look back at the official lion chaser's manifesto on page 2 if you need inspiration. But this is *your* manifesto. Get specific and get personal. Refuse to let impossible odds break your spirit. Instead, allow impossible odds to strengthen your resolve as you fight for your God-given dreams.

my
LION CHASER'S
MANIFESTO

SETTING LIFE GOALS

On a rainy afternoon in 1940, a teenager named John Goddard pulled out a piece of paper and wrote *My Life List* at the top of it. In one afternoon, he managed to write down 127 life goals. By the time he turned fifty, he had accomplished 108 of them. And these were no garden-variety goals!

- Milk a poisonous snake

- Learn jujitsu

- Study primitive culture in Borneo

- Run a mile in five minutes

- Retrace the travels of Marco Polo and Alexander the Great

- Photograph Victoria Falls in Rhodesia

- Climb Mt. Kilimanjaro

- Build a telescope

- Read the Bible from cover to cover

- Circumnavigate the globe

- Publish an article in *National Geographic* magazine

- Play the flute and violin

- Learn French, Spanish, and Arabic

Honestly, I would have counted French, Spanish, and Arabic as three separate goals! And learning to play the flute and violin as two. But that's just me.

My favorite Goddard goal may be one he never achieved: *visit the moon*. He set that goal long before we figured out how to escape the Earth's atmosphere. That's aiming for the stars, literally!

John Goddard did not accomplish every goal he set. He never *climbed Mount Everest* and his quest to *visit every country in the world* fell a few countries short. But I think it's safe to say that Goddard would not have done half of the things he did if he hadn't set those goals in the first place! And that's the point of goal-setting. Simply put, you won't accomplish any of the goals you do not set.

I discovered John Goddard's list when I was twenty-nine, and it inspired me to create a life goal list of my own. I came up with 25 goals on my first attempt. Over the years, I have added to and subtracted from that list. When I wrote *The Circle Maker* in 2011, I included 115 life goals. In this planner, I've pared that list down to 100. Before I share my list, let me outline the seven steps to setting life goals to help you get started.

1. START WITH PRAYER

Prayer is the perfect way to jump-start the process of goal setting. Why? Because a goal set in the context of prayer is much more likely to align with God's plans and purposes. And if the goal doesn't align, it's not worth setting in the first place. What you'll discover is that praying is a form of dreaming and dreaming is a form of praying. The more you pray, the more you dream. And the more you dream, the more you have to pray. The net result will be some God-ordained, God-sized goals. I also recommend a personal retreat or even a period of fasting. If you can, get away for a weekend. Maybe even forget your phone! And remember this:

change of pace + change of place = change of perspective

2. CHECK YOUR MOTIVES

If you set selfish goals, you'd be better off if you don't accomplish them! That's why you need to check your motives up front. You need to take a long look in the mirror and make sure you're going after the right goals for the right reasons. You've got to examine and cross-examine your goals to make sure your motives aren't out of whack. When I started setting goals, I had quite a few that were, in retrospect, quite selfish. When it came to financial goals, for example, I was more focused on "getting" goals than "giving" goals. What did I do? I turned those getting goals into giving goals, and it changed my focus. The other thing I did was add a relational component to many of my life goals. I cannot accomplish many of my goals by myself, and that is by design. Why? Because I don't want to cross the finish line by myself.

3. THINK IN CATEGORIES

It is hard to pull life goals out of thin air, so I would actually recommend looking at other people's lists. Don't cut-and-paste all their goals onto your list, but it's a great way of getting your own ideas. Another trick of the trade is thinking in categories. I currently have three categories: Relational, Influential, and Experiential. But you can subdivide your list in any way you choose (for instance, you could create categories such as Financial Goals, Travel Goals, Relational Goals, etc.). For the record, I don't have a category for "spiritual" because I'd like to believe that all of them are! Some of them are more obviously spiritual, like *taking each of my children on a mission trip* or *reading the Bible from cover to cover in seven different translations*, but *running a marathon* was a spiritual experience as well. Why? Because I ran it to celebrate God healing my asthma after forty years of fighting it. I've also discovered that any goal that cultivates *physical discipline* will cultivate *spiritual discipline* too.

4. BE SPECIFIC

If a goal isn't measurable, you have no way of knowing whether or not you've accomplished it. Losing weight isn't a goal if you don't have a target weight within a target timeline. How many pounds do you want to lose? When do you want to reach your goal weight? Goals are dreams with deadlines. One of the ways I've increased the specificity of my goals is by attaching ages to them. For example, I want to run a *triathlon* in my sixties. That goal is time-stamped. I've also added nuances that make my goals more fun and meaningful. I don't just want to go to a Super Bowl; I want to *go to a Super Bowl with Josiah.* It was incredibly difficult attaching numbers to some of my giving and writing goals, but I decided that it was better to aim high and fall short than to aim low and hit the target. And for the record, it's okay to make *revisions* to our *visions*.

5. WRITE THEM DOWN

I live by a little mantra: *The shortest pencil is longer than the longest memory.* If you haven't written down your goals, you haven't really set them. Or maybe I should say, you haven't set them in stone. Something powerful happens when you verbalize a goal. That act of verbalization is an act of faith. But there is something about the act of writing that produces clarity and creates accountability. In a sense, the *Chase the Lion Weekly Planner* doubles as a dream journal. And it won't just help you chase your goals; it will give you a paper trail so you can look back and see how you got there! That way, you can steward your experience by sharing it with someone else!

6. INCLUDE OTHERS

I used to have lots of individual goals, but I have replaced most of them with shared goals. Nothing cements a relationship like a shared goal. Goals are like relational glue. And God set the standard with the Great Commission. When you "co-mission" with another person by going after a goal, you have someone there to help you up if you fall down. It also doubles your joy when you accomplish the goal. One of the experiential goals I've checked off my list was to *spend a night on Catalina Island with Lora*. I fell in love with that idyllic island off the coast of California when I first visited it in 1999. I strolled the streets and toured the town. I even went *parasailing* over the Pacific. It was a magical day, but I did all those things by myself. All day I kept thinking to myself: *I wish Lora were here*. It took about fifteen years, but I finally checked that goal off the list when Lora and I experienced it together a few years ago. And it was twice as fun! A lot of my life goals revolve around my family, tailored to the unique personalities and passions of my wife and my children. When we experience those things together, shared goals turn into shared memories.

7. CELEBRATE ALONG THE WAY

When I check a life goal off my list, I tend to move on immediately to the next one. Why? Because I have a driven personality. That drivenness is what fuels me to go after goals and accomplish them, but I've learned the importance of celebrating along the way. In 1 Samuel 7:12, the prophet Samuel sets up an altar and names it *Ebenezer*. It means: *hitherto the Lord has helped us*. Translation: so far so God. When you accomplish a God-ordained goal, it is an Ebenezer moment. Find a way to celebrate it and commemorate it. Maybe even build an altar! Whenever I write a new book, our family celebrates with a special meal on the day the book is released. It's the way we "stop and smell the roses," or in this instance, whatever kind of food we are about to eat. When you accomplish a goal, celebrate it by sharing a meal, throwing a party, or building an altar.

• • •

My life goals are not listed in any particular order. I recognize that some of them may seem grandiose while others seem trivial. But life goals are as unique as we are. Note that the goals I've *italicized* have been accomplished.

MARK'S 100 LIFE GOALS[*]

RELATIONAL GOALS

1. Celebrate 50th wedding anniversary

2. Live long enough to dedicate my great-grandchildren

3. *Celebrate an anniversary in Italy*

4. *Celebrate an anniversary in the Caribbean*

5. Take each child on a mission trip

6. *Coach a sports team for each child*

7. Pay for our grandchildren's college educations

8. *Create a family foundation*

9. Leave an inheritance for our children

10. Write an autobiography

11. *Create a discipleship covenant*

12. *Take each child on a rite of passage pilgrimage*

13. *Create a family coat of arms*

14. Research our family genealogy

15. Find and visit an ancestor's grave in Sweden

16. Take our grandchildren to a state fair

17. Go on a camping trip with our grandchildren

18. Celebrate a family reunion in Alexandria, Minnesota

19. Write 25+ nonfiction books

20. Pastor one church for 40+ years

21. Help 1,000,000 dads disciple their sons

22. *Speak at a college commencement*

23. *Speak at an NFL chapel*

24. *Write a* New York Times *bestseller*

25. *Write a novel*

26. *Start a mentoring group for pastors*

27. Create a conference for writers

28. *Create a conference for pastors*

29. *Teach a college course*

30. Lead National Community Church to 10,000+ in weekly attendance

31. Baptize 3,000 people in the same place at the same time

32. Build an orphanage in Ethiopia

33. *Get a doctoral degree*

34. Start a chain of coffeehouses that give their net profits to kingdom causes

35. Help plant 100+ churches

36. Make a movie

37. *Host a radio or television program*

38. Be debt-free by 55

39. Give back every penny we've earned from National Community Church

40. Live off 10% and give 90%

41. Give away $5+ million

42. Lead National Community Church to give $25,000,000 to missions

EXPERIENTIAL GOALS

43. *Take Summer to a Broadway play*

44. *Hike the Inca Trail to Machu Picchu with Parker*

45. *Go to a Super Bowl with Josiah*

46. *Spend a night on Catalina Island with Lora*

47. *Go paragliding with Parker*

48. *Go cliff jumping*

49. Take one of my kids to a film festival

50. *Learn how to snowboard*

51. Learn how to surf

52. *Take a helicopter ride over the Grand Canyon*

53. *Take a rafting trip through the Grand Canyon*

54. *Take a three-month sabbatical*

55. Do a silent retreat at a monastery

56. Go on an overnight canoe trip with one of my kids

57. Drive a race car with one of my kids

58. Read the Bible from cover to cover in seven translations

59. Take a hot-air balloon ride

60. *Go horseback riding as a family*

61. Spend a night in a treehouse hotel

62. Hike the Camino de Santiago in Spain

63. Run with the bulls in Pamplona

64. *Play a round of golf at St. Andrews in Scotland*

65. Do a stand-up comedy routine

66. Take Lora to the Oscars

67. Go to a TED conference

68. Retrace one of Paul's missionary journeys

69. Take an RV vacation as a family

70. *Hike to the top of Half Dome*

71. *Stay at the Ahwahnee Lodge in Yosemite*

72. *Visit the Biltmore Mansion*

73. *Stay at Old Faithful Inn at Yellowstone*

74. *Hike to Inspiration Point at Lake Jenny*

75. *Go to a rodeo out west*

76. Climb to the Cliff Churches in Lalibela, Ethiopia

77. Visit the Meteora Monasteries in Greece

78. Go on an African safari

79. See a kangaroo in Australia

80. Snorkel the Barrier Reef

81. *Kiss Lora on top of the Eiffel Tower*

82. See the aurora borealis

83. Go kayaking in Alaska

84. *Visit the Castle Church in Wittenberg, Germany*

85. Take a boat cruise down the Rhine River

86. Ride a gondola in Venice

87. *See the sunrise on Cadillac Mountain*

88. *Straddle the equator*

89. *See the Blue Grotto in Capri*

90. Visit the Parthenon in Athens, Greece

91. *Take a carriage ride through Central Park*

92. *Stay at the Grand Hotel on Mackinac Island*

93. *Hike the Grand Canyon from rim to rim*

94. Climb a 14er

95. Swim the Escape from Alcatraz with Summer

96. *Run a triathlon with Parker*

97. Bike a century with Josiah

98. *Run a triathlon*

99. Run a triathlon in my sixties

100. *Run a marathon*

my
100 LIFE GOALS

NOTES

MARK BATTERSON is the *New York Times* best-selling author of more than a dozen books, including *The Circle Maker*, *In a Pit with a Lion on a Snowy Day*, and *Chase the Lion*. He is the lead pastor of National Community Church, one of the most innovative and influential churches in America. One church with eight campuses, NCC also owns and operates Ebenezers Coffeehouse, the Miracle Theatre, and the DC Dream Center. Mark holds a Doctor of Ministry degree from Regent University. He and his wife, Lora, have three children and live on Capitol Hill.

Twitter: @markbatterson | Instagram: @markbatterson | Facebook: markbatterson

Chase the Lion Weekly Planner

ISBN 978-0-525-65342-4

Cover design by Danielle Deschenes; cover image by Keith Ladzinski | Getty; claw marks courtesy of Shutterstock © Maryna Stamatova

Published in association with the literary agency of The Fedd Agency, Inc., P.O. Box 341973, Austin, TX 78734

Published in the United States by Multnomah, an imprint of the Crown Publishing Group, a division of Penguin Random House LLC, New York.

MULTNOMAH® and its mountain colophon are registered trademarks of Penguin Random House LLC.

Selected material originally appeared in Chase the Lion by Mark Batterson, published by Multnomah, an imprint of the Crown Publishing Group, a division of Penguin Random House LLC, New York, in 2016.

Printed in China
2019—First Edition

10 9 8 7 6 5 4 3 2 1

SPECIAL SALES
Most Multnomah books are available at special quantity discounts when purchased in bulk by corporations, organizations, and special-interest groups. Custom imprinting or excerpting can also be done to fit special needs. For information, please e-mail specialmarketscms@penguinrandomhouse.com or call 1-800-603-7051.